AZTECS

VS.

SPARTANS

45th Parallel Press

Published in the United States of America by Cherry Lake Publishing
Ann Arbor, Michigan
www.cherrylakepublishing.com

Reading Adviser: Marla Conn, MS, Ed., Literacy specialist, Read-Ability, Inc.
Book Designer: Melinda Millward

Photo Credits: © DM7/Shutterstock.com, back cover, 16; © fitopardo.com/Getty Images, cover, 5; © Riznychen-ko Oksana/Shutterstock.com, cover, 5, 12; ©Moment/Getty Images, 6; ©Diego Gomez / Alamy Stock Photo, 9; © MatiasEnElMundo/istock, 10; © mark turner/Dreamstime.com, 15; © GraphicsRF/Shutterstock.com, 19, 20; © Anna Om/Shutterstock.com, 19; © vectortatu/Shutterstock.com, 20; © Serhii Bobyk/Shutterstock.com, 21; © duncan1890/istock, 23; © draco77vector/Shutterstock.com, 24; © maewshooter/Shutterstock.com, 25; © MR . JOE 666/Shutterstock.com, 25; ©Diego Gomez / Alamy Stock Photo, 27; © Lucian Bogdan/Dreamstime.com, 29

Graphic Element Credits: © studiostoks/Shutterstock.com, back cover, multiple interior pages; © infostocker/ Shutterstock.com, back cover, multiple interior pages; © mxbfilms/Shutterstock.com, front cover; © MF production/Shutterstock.com, front cover, multiple interior pages; © AldanNi/Shutterstock.com, front cover, multiple interior pages; © Andrii Symonenko/Shutterstock.com, front cover, multiple interior pages; © acidmit/ Shutterstock.com, front cover, multiple interior pages; © manop/Shutterstock.com, multiple interior pages; © Lina Kalina/Shutterstock.com, multiple interior pages; © mejorana/Shutterstock.com, multiple interior pages; © NoraVector/Shutterstock.com, multiple interior pages; © Smirnov Viacheslav/Shutterstock.com, multiple interior pages; © Piotr Urakau/Shutterstock.com, multiple interior pages; © IMOGI graphics/Shutterstock.com, multiple interior pages; © jirawat phueksriphan/Shutterstock.com, multiple interior pages

45th Parallel Press is an imprint of Cherry Lake Publishing.

Library of Congress Cataloging-in-Publication Data

Names: Loh-Hagan, Virginia, author.
Title: Aztecs vs. Spartans / by Virginia Loh-Hagan.
Other titles: Aztecs versus Spartans
Description: [Ann Arbor : Cherry Lake Publishing, 2019] | Series: Battle royale : lethal warriors |
    Audience: Grade 4 to 6. | Includes bibliographical references and index.
Identifiers: LCCN 2019003642| ISBN 9781534147683 (hardcover) | ISBN 9781534150546 (pbk.) |
    ISBN 9781534151970 (hosted ebook) | ISBN 9781534149113 (PDF)
Subjects: LCSH: Aztecs—Warfare—Juvenile literature. | Sparta (Extinct city)—Juvenile literature. |
    Imaginary wars and battles—Juvenile literature. | Soldiers—Juvenile literature.
Classification: LCC F1219.76.W37 L64 2019 | DDC 938/.9—dc23
LC record available at https://lccn.loc.gov/2019003642

Printed in the United States of America
Corporate Graphics

About the Author

Dr. Virginia Loh-Hagan is an author, university professor, former classroom teacher, and curriculum designer. She works at San Diego State University (SDSU). The SDSU mascot is the Aztecs. She lives in San Diego with her very tall husband and very naughty dogs. To learn more about her, visit www.virginialoh.com.

Table of Contents

Introduction...4

Aztecs 6

Spartans.. 12

Choose Your Battleground 18

Fight On!.. 22

And the Victor Is. 28

Consider This! 32
Learn More!... 32
Glossary 32
Index 32

Introduction

Imagine a battle between Aztecs and Spartans. Who would win? Who would lose?

Enter the world of *Battle Royale: Lethal **Warriors**!* Warriors are fighters. This is a fight to the death! The last team standing is the **victor**! Victors are winners. They get to live.

Opponents are fighters who compete against each other. They challenge each other. They fight with everything they've got. They use weapons. They use their special skills. They use their powers.

They're not fighting for prizes. They're not fighting for honor. They're not fighting for their countries. They're fighting for their lives. Victory is their only option.

Let the games begin!

In real life,
nobody really
wins in a war.

AZTECS

The Aztec language is called Nahuatl.

Aztec warriors were from Mexico. War was a part of Aztec life. Their gods were always fighting. The sun and moon fought every day. To the Aztecs, fighting was like breathing.

They fought to grow their lands. They fought to get resources. They fought to keep people in order. They fought to provide human **sacrifices**. Sacrifices are offerings to gods. Aztecs took prisoners. They killed these prisoners. They gave them to their Aztec gods. They wanted to make gods happy. They wanted to make sure the sun rose every morning. They thought human blood was needed to do this.

There were different types of fighters. Eagle Warriors were **scouts**. Scouts were like spies. They went ahead. They got information. They helped plan attacks. They wore helmets with eagle feathers and heads.

Jaguar Warriors were the best fighters. They wore jaguar skins. The **Shorn** Ones were the top warriors. They were the most feared. Shorn means shaved. The Shorn Ones had shaved heads. They had one long braid. The braid was on the backs of their heads. The Shorn Ones painted bright colors on their faces. They never stepped back in battle. They were like special forces.

Common people could also fight. They formed their own fighting teams. They were led by each city's leader.

Aztec warriors could rise in their ranks.

Aztec warriors got rewarded for capturing prisoners. They had different weapons. They used spears and swords. They used sharp rocks as blades. They used slings. They shot out rocks and stones. They used bows and arrows. They used clubs or bats. They used shields. They used poisoned darts. They wore thick cloths for protection. This let them move quickly.

Aztecs didn't have armies. Warriors were called as needed. All Aztec rulers were warriors. All Aztec men became warriors. They started training at age 15. They learned fighting skills. They learned to use weapons. They were always ready to fight.

FUN FACTS ABOUT AZTECS

- Aztec warriors played ullamaliztli. This was a ball game. The ball was rubber. It was 9 pounds (4 kilograms). Teams faced each other. They tried to get the ball through stone hoops. The ball couldn't touch the ground. Players couldn't touch the ball with their hands. In some games, losers' heads were cut off. They were sacrificed to the gods.

- Aztecs thought giving birth was like a battle. Mothers were seen as warriors. Having babies could be dangerous. Some Aztec women died giving birth. They were treated like warriors who died in war.

- When Aztec warriors died, they were sent to a special afterlife. Their souls helped the war god fight darkness. They helped the sun rise each day. They did this for 4 years. Then, they returned to Earth as birds.

- Bernardino de Sahagún was a Spanish monk. He lived among the Aztecs. He studied them for 50 years. He learned their language. He wrote a book about the Aztecs. He died in 1590.

SPARTANS

A popular saying was "One Spartan was worth several men of any other state."

Spartans were warriors from ancient Greece. Ancient Greece was made up many different **city-states**. City-states are like nations. These city-states fought against each other. They fought for land. They fought for resources. Sparta was the largest and most powerful nation. Sparta was a military state.

Preparing for war started with births. The goal of marriage was to make male babies. Strong women were matched with strong men. Fast women were matched with fast men. Spartans wanted healthy babies.

Weak male babies were left to die. Boys started training at age 7. They grew up to be Spartan soldiers. They replaced soldiers who died in battle. Men with no children were shamed. Men with lots of children were celebrated.

Military training was tough. Spartans joined the military at age 20. They trained until age 30. They learned to fight. They learned to use weapons. They learned war strategies. They fought in fake battles. They boxed. They wrestled. They played sports and games. They competed a lot. They were pushed to be winners. They practiced many drills. They were **disciplined**. Disciplined means in control.

Spartans had to be hardy. They learned survival skills. They were given little to eat. They were given little to wear. They slept in the cold. They were forced to stay awake. They learned to handle any and all situations.

Sparta was the only Greek city without a city wall. Some said Sparta had a wall of men.

They used several weapons. They used spears. They used knives. They used swords. They used large shields. They wore metal **armor**. Armor is body covering used for protection. Spartans wore helmets. They wore leg guards. They wore capes to keep warm.

In war, Spartans marched. They carried their weapons. They traveled with their slaves. Slaves carried their supplies.

Spartan warriors had a code of honor. They valued loyalty to Sparta above all. They served until age 60. They never quit. They never laid down their weapons. They were willing to die in battle. But they fought to live. Gravestones were given to warriors who died in battles. They were also given to women who died in childbirth.

FUN FACTS ABOUT SPARTANS

- Spartan women had more freedoms than other ancient Greek women. They could own land. They were educated. They practiced sports. They had to be strong to have strong sons.

- Men could marry at age 30. Women could marry at age 20. They couldn't live together until men were done with military training.

- Cynisca was born in 440 BCE. She was a Spartan princess. She competed in the ancient Olympic games. She was the first woman to win.

- Spartans enslaved the Helots. Helots were Greeks who lived in Messenia. They were farm slaves. They made food for Spartans. Spartans were in fear of slave uprisings. So, they started a war with Helots every fall. The krypteia was a Spartan secret police. They hunted and killed the strongest Helots.

- Spartans valued bravery. Cowards were shunned. They had to sew patches on their clothes. This was so everyone knew they were cowards.

CHOOSE YOUR BATTLEGROUND

Aztecs and Spartans are fierce fighters. They're well-matched. Both groups have trained since childhood. Both groups are loyal. They fight for their nations. Both groups aren't afraid to die. But they do have different ways of fighting. So, choose your battleground carefully!

Battleground #1: Sea

• Aztecs live in Central America. They're surrounded by water on both sides. Their capital city is on a small island in a lake. Aztecs know how to make and use small boats. They made waterways.

• Spartans are better land fighters. But Sparta is on a peninsula. Peninsulas are pieces of land. They're almost completely surrounded by water. They project out into a body of water.

Aztecs built beautiful buildings.

Battleground #2: Land

• Aztecs work best on land. They use the land. They practice **guerilla warfare**. This means they hide. It means they **ambush**. Ambush is a sneak attack.

• Spartans are great fighters on battlefields. They march over different types of landforms. They travel great distances.

Battleground #3: Mountains

• Aztecs live in Mexico. Mexico is a land of extremes. It has high mountains. It has deep canyons. It has deserts. It has rainforests. Mountains cover most of Mexico.

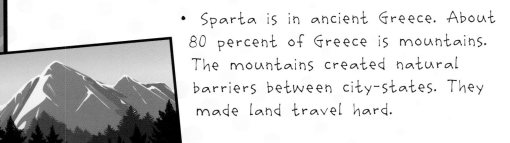

• Sparta is in ancient Greece. About 80 percent of Greece is mountains. The mountains created natural barriers between city-states. They made land travel hard.

ARMED AND DANGEROUS: WEAPONS

Aztecs: Aztecs didn't have metal weapons. They didn't know how to heat metals to change their shape. So, they used obsidian. Obsidian is a sharp stone. It's like glass. It's volcanic rock. The most famous ancient Aztec weapon was macuahuitl. Macuahuitl means "hungry wood." It was a flat wooden paddle. Its blade was obsidian. It was sharp. It could chop off a horse's head in one blow.

Spartans: Spartan warriors used a dory. A dory was a spear. It was between 7 and 9 feet (2 and 2.7 meters) long. One hand would hold the dory. The other would hold a shield. The dory was made of hard wood. The blade on the main end was sharp. It was made of iron. The other end of the dory had small blades. They balanced the spears. They were backups in case the main blade broke.

FIGHT ON!

The battle begins! Aztecs and Spartans meet up. They're in a valley. Valleys are between hills or mountains. They're areas of low land.

Move 1:

Spartans take off their red capes. They get in phalanx formation. A phalanx is a military move. Formation is an organized line. Spartans use this move to attack and defend. They form eight single lines. There are 12 men in each line. The lines are right behind each other. Spartans stand close together. They hold their shields in front. They make a tight line of shields. They lower their long spears forward. They move forward at the same time.

Many Aztecs were killed by European sicknesses.

Move 2:

Aztecs come forward. They're wearing animal skins. They bang drums. They shout. They blow shell trumpets. They play bone flutes. They're trying to confuse and scare the Spartans. They throw themselves into the phalanx. Some Aztecs are on higher ground. They sling rocks. They blow out poisoned darts.

Move 3:

Some Spartans scatter. Some fall down. When Spartans get out of line, other Spartans move up. They replace each other. They keep marching forward. They move around together. Their long spears pierce into the Aztecs. Aztecs' war clothes don't protect them.

Spartans learned to read maps. They also learned reading, math, and the arts.

LIFE SOURCE: FOOD FOR BATTLE

Aztecs: Aztec warriors ate chia seeds. The seeds gave them energy. They helped them during long periods of battle. They helped them on long trips. They held seeds in their hands. Chia means "strength" in the Mayan language. Chia seeds taste nutty. They take poisons out of the body. They help people lose weight. They control blood sugars. They keep the heart healthy. Aztecs ate chia seeds every day. They ground them into flour. They pressed them for oil. They mixed them in their drinks.

Spartans: Spartans ate simple meals. They ate a lot of meat. A popular dish was black soup. Black soup was made from boiling pig legs. Pig's blood, salt, and vinegar were added. It gave Spartans strength. It made them full. An Italian ate the soup. He said, "Now I know why the Spartans do not fear death."

Move 4:

Aztecs pull back. They run away. Spartans keep moving forward. Aztecs trick the Spartans. The night before, they had built **trenches**. Trenches are long, deep ditches. Aztecs put sharp poles in the trenches. Spartans move forward. Some men fall. They get stabbed.

Move 5:

The Spartan phalanx keeps moving. They march over the fallen men. They push through with their shields. The first row aims to stab arms, throats, and eyes. The second row throws their spears.

Move 6:

Aztecs use ropes. They get the hurt men. They'll keep them alive. They'll use them for human sacrifices. They try to break up the phalanx. They pull away soldiers at the ends. They fight them one-on-one.

Aztecs killed thousands of people a year for their human sacrifices. Most were war prisoners.

AND THE VICTOR IS . . .

What are their next moves?
Who do you think would win?

Aztecs could win if:

- They break through Spartans' military lines. Aztecs are good fighters. But they're not as organized as Spartans.
- They killed soldiers instead of capturing them. They need to decrease the Spartan army. They need to get rid of soldiers.
- They do more sneak attacks. They hit and run. They spy. Spartans think this type of fighting is weak.

Spartans could win if:

- They avoid getting captured. Aztecs use humans for sacrifices.
- They use metal. Their armor and weapons are stronger than the Aztecs' war gear.

Dead Spartan soldiers were placed on their shield. They were carried home this way.

Aztecs: Top Champion

Montezuma II was born around 1466. He was born in Mexico City. As a kid, he loved learning. His favorite subject was religion. He became a priest. At age 36, he became king of the Aztecs. The Aztec Empire included Mexico, Nicaragua, and Honduras. Montezuma was worried about ruling a big empire. He had to maintain his power. He created a class system. He created religious schools. He was also a great warrior. He led several battles against rebels. Conquered people had to pay the king. Montezuma made people pay him twice as much as they did before. His people gave him gold, gems, food, and humans. Hernan Cortes came in 1520. Cortes was a Spanish explorer. He took Montezuma prisoner. Montezuma gave in. He lost his people's respect. He tried to talk to them. People threw rocks at him. Montezuma died 3 days later. He was the last Aztec emperor.

Spartans: Top Champion

King Leonidas ruled Sparta. He was a great military leader. He trained to be a Spartan soldier. He died in 480 BCE. He died in the Battle of Thermopylae. Thermopylae was the gateway to Greece. Persian armies came to invade. They wanted to grow their empire. Leonidas fought against the Persians. He led a small Greek army. He resisted the large Persian army. He fought them for 2 days. He knew he was losing. So, he ordered most of his men to leave. He saved their lives. But he stayed to fight. He only had 300 soldiers with him. He fought to the last man. He fought until his own death. He lost the battle. But he became a war hero. He held the Persians off for several days. He didn't quit. Many stories were told about him. People said Spartans never surrendered. Surrender means to give up.

Consider This!

THINK ABOUT IT!

- How are the Aztecs and Spartans alike? How are they different? Are they more alike or different? Why do you think so?
- If the Aztecs and Spartans lived at the same time, do you think they would've fought each other? If they did, who would've won? Why do you think so?
- Read the 45th Parallel Press book about Immortals. Spartans and Immortals fought in real life. Why did they fight? What happened? Who won?
- Learn more about the Aztecs' real enemies. Who were they? How did they fight? Why did they fight? Did Aztecs win or lose?
- What's left of the Aztec and Spartan cultures? What are they like today? How did they change over the years?
- Both Aztecs and Spartans believed in gods and goddesses. Who were their war gods and goddesses? How did these gods and goddesses influence their fighting styles?

LEARN MORE!

- Clint, Marc. *Aztec Warriors*. Minneapolis, MN: Bellwether Media, 2012.
- Dinzeo, Paul. *Spartans*. Minneapolis, MN: Bellwether Media, 2012.
- Lee, Adrienne. *Aztec Warriors*. North Mankato, MN: Capstone Press, 2014.
- Matthews, Rupert. *Spartans*. New York, NY: Gareth Stevens Publishing, 2016.

GLOSSARY

ambush (AM-bush) to do a surprise attack
armor (AHR-mur) body covering used for protection
city-states (SIT-ee-states) independently governed nations in ancient Greece
disciplined (DIS-uh-plind) showing a controlled form of behavior
formation (for-MAY-shuhn) a formal arrangement used in military strategies
guerilla warfare (guh-RIL-uh WOR-fair) irregular military actions, like hit-and-run tactics, carried out by small forces
opponents (uh-POH-nuhnts) groups who compete against each other

phalanx (FAY-lanks) a group of armed troops standing or moving in close formation
sacrifices (SAK-ruh-fise-iz) offerings to gods
scouts (SKOUTS) people who go ahead of an army to survey the area
shorn (SHORN) shaved, sheared, or cut hair
trenches (TRENCH-iz) long, deep ditches used in warfare
valley (VAL-ee) low land between hills or mountains
victor (VIK-tur) the winner
warriors (WOR-ee-urz) fighters

INDEX

Aztecs, 30
  battlegrounds, 18–20
  battles, 22–26
  fun facts about, 11
  how they win, 28
  types of fighters, 8
  weapons, 10, 21
  who they were, 6–11
  why they fought, 7

battlegrounds, 18–20
battles, 22–26

code of honor, 16

food, 25

Greece, 13

Leonidas, King, 31

Mexico, 7
Montezuma II, 30

opponents, 4

Spartans, 31
  battlegrounds, 18–20
  battles, 22–26
  fun facts about, 17
  how they win, 29
  training, 13–14
  weapons, 16, 21
  who they were, 12–17

victors, 4

weapons, 10, 16, 21